Parliame... generous br... ...to vote itself ... existence. On 1 M... ...of Union was passed. The S... poet Robert Burns later wro... of th... ..t, "We're bought and sold for English gold, such a parcel of rogues in ...nation!"

The first article of the Act of Un...n declared "That the two Kingdoms of England and Scotland shall up... the first day of May… be united into one Kingdom by the name of G...at Britain." The Act also described the flag that this new country wou...d use, combining the diagonal white cross of St Andrew, and the red cross of St George. This new national flag was nicknamed the **'Union Jack'**.

The Hanoverian succession

Queen Anne had been ill for many years, and died in 1714. Her doctor wrote, "I believe sleep was never more welcome to a weary traveller than death was to her". So, Parliament set about searching Europe for Anne's closest surviving Protestant relative to be her successor. The answer was found in the shape of Georg Ludwig, the 54-year-old ruler of a small German state called Hanover. He just happened to be the great-grandson of James I.

Georg Ludwig arrived in London on 18 September with a procession of 260 horse-drawn carriages, and was crowned George I of Great Britain a month later. Britain now had a new royal family, known as the **Hanoverians**.

For many people, it was a strange sight. There were 57 Catholic descendents of the Stuarts across Europe with a better claim to the English throne than George I. Before being plucked from obscurity to become King, George I had only visited England once in his life. He spoke no English and took very little interest in the country, preferring to spend his time playing cards, visiting Germany, and entertaining his two mistresses. They were nicknamed the elephant and the maypole because one was very fat, and the other was very thin.

Fact

George I was famous for his temper. While he was Elector of Hanover, he had found out his wife was unfaithful, so he locked her in a tower for the rest of her life.

Painting of George I, who went from ruling a small German state to becoming King of Great Britain in 1714

Check your understanding

1. Why were many people in Scotland opposed to the Act of Settlement?
2. Why did the English Parliament propose in 1703 that England and Scotland become one country?
3. How did the English Parliament manage to win round the Scots into supporting the Act of Union?
4. Why did George I become king in 1714 when 57 people across Europe had a better claim to the throne?
5. Where had George I ruled before he was crowned King of Great Britain?

Parliamentary government

Although George I was king, he knew almost nothing about how to rule Britain. For this reason he relied on his **ministers**, normally Members of Parliament, to make decisions on his behalf.

Britain's first Prime Minister, Sir Robert Walpole

After an unhappy century of absolutist monarchs causing disagreements and wars, this new situation suited Parliament very nicely. From now on, the monarch reigned but ministers ruled.

The first Prime Minister

Robert Walpole was a wealthy farmer from Norfolk and a Member of Parliament. He weighed 20 stone, loved drinking and eating, and had ambitions to become the most powerful politician in Britain. Walpole's political career took off after an economic crash called **the South Sea Bubble** (see box). Walpole was made Paymaster General and successfully restored Britain's economy, becoming George I's favourite minister as a result.

Walpole was not an honest man. He would bribe other politicians to get his way. As a young man he even spent six months imprisoned in the Tower of London for corruption! One of his favourite sayings was that "all men have their price". However, Walpole was a popular figure and good at his job.

10 Downing Street, London, England

In 1721, Walpole was given three of the key jobs in British politics: First Lord of the Treasury, Chancellor of the Exchequer and Leader of the **House of Commons**. This made him the most important minister in the King's Government, so people would refer to him as the **'prime' minister**. The king gave him a house in London to live in, and selected number 10 on a new development near Parliament called 'Downing Street'. Walpole recommended that the house should forever remain the property of whoever held his position. To this day the Prime Minister of Great Britain lives at number **10 Downing Street**.

Parliamentary government

In 1727 King George I died, and his son George II became king. George II spoke a bit more English, but with a heavy German accent. He thought Walpole had become too powerful as Prime Minister, and tried to replace him. However, Walpole promised George II that, if he was kept as Prime Minister, he would increase the king's allowance. Since the Glorious Revolution, Parliament controlled the monarch's annual allowance – something known as the 'power of the purse'. So, George II decided to let Walpole keep his job.

Fact

In 1755 George II visited Hanover and considered not returning to Britain because he was so angry at the growing power of Parliament. He complained, "Ministers are the kings in this country, I am nothing there."

As Prime Minister, Walpole had two ambitions: to stay out of any foreign wars, and to keep taxes low. He succeeded, and Britain grew wealthy as her foreign trade flourished. Walpole once boasted to Queen Caroline, the wife of George II, "Madam, there are 50 000 men slain this year in Europe, and not one Englishman".

Painting of the Prime Minister addressing the House of Commons, from the end of the eighteenth century

During the 20 years that Walpole was in power, he established **'parliamentary government'** in Great Britain. In theory the king could choose his government ministers, but in reality he could only choose those with the support of the most powerful party in Parliament. Parliament was, as it still is today, split into two 'Houses': the Commons and the Lords. Seats in the House of Commons went to Members of Parliament elected by the British public, though only a small minority of wealthy men had the vote. Most seats in the **House of Lords** passed down through generations of noble families along with hereditary titles, which were – in order of importance – Duke, Marquess, Earl, Viscount, and Baron.

By this time, two rival political parties had developed in Parliament, each with different ideas about how England should be governed. One party wanted to limit the power of the king and allow greater tolerance for religious groups. They were nicknamed **'Whigs'**—an old Scottish insult for Presbyterian rebels. The other group wanted to protect the power of the king and the Church of England. They were nicknamed **'Tories'**—an old Irish word for a Catholic outlaw.

The South Sea Bubble

The South Sea Bubble was one of the greatest economic disasters in British history. Exclusive rights to trade with Spanish colonies in South America were granted to the South Sea Company, and company **shares** became highly sought after. Over the spring of 1720, its share price increased by ten times, but then the bubble burst and the share price came crashing down.

Thousands of normal citizens who had invested in the company were made bankrupt overnight, company directors fled the country, and a spate of suicides took place. One government minister, Lord Stanhope, even died of a stroke during an angry debate in Parliament.

Check your understanding:

1. How did Robert Walpole become George I's favourite minister?
2. How was the role of Prime Minster established during Walpole's time in power?
3. How did the system of parliamentary government, established by Walpole, function?
4. Why did George II consider not returning from Hanover when he visited in 1755?
5. What caused the South Sea Bubble to take place?

Unit 6: Georgian Britain
Jacobite uprisings

Most people in Britain were by now happy with their new German kings, but a small group retained a passionate belief that the Stuart royal family should still be governing Britain.

These people called themselves **'Jacobites'**, a name taken from the Latin word for 'James'. They formed secret societies across England and Scotland, and plotted to overthrow the Hanoverian kings. In 1715, a small Jacobite rebellion failed to place James II's son, James Stuart, on the throne. But they kept on plotting – waiting for the right moment to act.

Bonnie Prince Charlie

By 1745 the British army was busy fighting the French in Europe, so the Jacobites spotted a chance. Support for the Stuart claim to the throne was strongest in the mountains and moors of the Scottish **Highlands**. Ancient **'clans'** ruled this part of Scotland, and each clan was led by a 'chief'. The clansmen were mostly poor Catholic farmers, but they were also fierce warriors who believed the 1707 Act of Union had robbed Scotland of its independence.

Painting of Bonnie Prince Charlie with two clan chiefs, completed in 1892

The Jacobites found a new hope in James Stuart's eldest son, Charles Edward Stuart, who was a charismatic and brave soldier. He was also very good looking, so his Highland supporters named him 'Bonnie Prince Charlie' – 'Bonnie' meaning good-looking in Scotland. Prince Charlie landed in Scotland in July 1745, and the Highland clans rushed to welcome him. They raised enough men to take Edinburgh, the capital city of Scotland, and routed the small British army in Scotland at the Battle of Prestonpans.

The Highlanders wore Scottish **tartan** and caps with white cockades, and armed themselves with traditional Scottish swords called **claymores**. With these soldiers, Prince Charlie won a series of victories in Scotland, and by November his 6000 men were marching south towards London. With most of his army fighting in France, King George II was terrified. He even loaded a boat on the Thames with treasure so that he could make an easy escape if Prince Charlie's army arrived in London.

Prince Charlie expected that England's Jacobites, who for years had held underground meetings and identified each other through secret symbols, would rush to his support when he invaded England. When the moment came, however, most were not brave enough to risk their lives. Prince Charlie marched as far south as Derby, but his soldiers grew disheartened about the lack of support from the English people. On 5 December 1745, the Jacobite army began its retreat back to the Scottish Highlands.

The Battle of Culloden

By now, George II had raised an army led by his son the Duke of Cumberland and put a price of £30 000 on Prince Charlie's head.

Cumberland's red-coated soldiers shadowed the retreating Jacobites to the Highlands of Scotland, where they met for a final battle at Culloden Moor in April 1746. Cumberland defeated the Jacobite army in less than an hour, tearing them apart with his cannons and cavalry.

Bonnie Prince Charlie escaped from the battlefield, and for weeks he hid in the moors of Scotland. According to legend, he was found by a young woman named Flora MacDonald who planned his escape. MacDonald disguised Prince Charlie as her Irish maid, and he took a boat to the Isle of Skye, and from there he escaped to France.

Prince Charlie lived the rest of his life in exile in Italy. The Stuart cause was dead, and the Hanoverians were safely established as Britain's royal family. Culloden remains the last ever battle to be fought on British soil.

Fact

Prince Charlie died in Rome on 31 January 1788 the anniversary of his great-great-grandfather Charles I's execution in 1649.

Contemporary painting of the Battle of Culloden

Suppression of the Highlands

The British Government wanted to make sure that no Jacobite rising could ever happen again. Cumberland hunted down and killed all of the remaining Jacobite soldiers with such savagery that he became known as 'the Butcher'. The British Government did not stop there. They made it illegal for Highlanders to wear their traditional dress of tartan and kilts, or to own weapons. The right of the chiefs to rule their own clans was abolished, and many Highland farmers were forced to move to the Scottish lowlands, or emigrate to America.

A large barracks named **Fort George** was built outside Inverness so that the British army could keep a watchful eye on their troublesome fellow countrymen north of the border. From now on, the Scottish Highlands were firmly under the control of the British Government.

Memorial to the Jacobites, at Glenfinnan, Highlands, Scotland

Check your understanding:

1. Why did Jacobites oppose the Hanoverian kings?
2. Why did many of Scotland's highland clans support Bonnie Prince Charlie?
3. Why did Bonnie Prince Charlie's army retreat back to Scotland in December 1745?
4. What happened at the Battle of Culloden?
5. How did the British government ensure that no Jacobite rising could ever happen again in Scotland?

Georgian aristocracy

Parliamentary government in Georgian Britain may have weakened the power of the monarch, but power did not move to the people.

Instead, power became increasingly concentrated in the hands of Britain's nobility, leading many historians to call the 18th century the 'Age of **Aristocracy'**. There were 173 **peers** in the House of Lords in 1700, and the great majority of government ministers came from this closed circle of titled landowners. England's first 10 Prime Ministers included three dukes, one marquess, two earls, and two who became earls during their lifetime.

Powerful families such as the Temples dominated English politics: Earl Temple and all four of his brothers served as members of Parliament, with one – George Grenville – becoming Prime Minister. Meanwhile, their sister Hester married William Pitt, who later became Prime Minister and the Earl of Chatham, and whose son, Pitt the Younger, also served as Prime Minister.

When a peer had no sons to inherit his title, it would become extinct, so the king regularly had to create new peerages. However, breaking into this class from a humble background was almost impossible: of the 229 peerages created between 1700 and 1800, only 23 had no previous connection with the aristocracy. Though they sat in the House of Lords, the aristocracy still held influence over elections to the House of Commons. MPs in the Commons were often related by birth or marriage to the aristocracy, and in 1715, 224 of the 558 members of the House of Commons were the sons of MPs.

The Georgian aristocracy grew increasingly wealthy during this period, often acquiring more land from the gentry, whose wealth was in decline. Aristocratic stately homes, such as Castle Howard and Blenheim Palace, remain some of the most extravagant buildings in Britain. Wentworth Woodhouse in Yorkshire, home to the 2nd Marquess of Rockingham (who became Prime Minister in 1765), is Britain's largest stately home, with over 300 rooms.

Painting of Mr and Mrs Andrews, a wealthy couple from the landed gentry, completed in 1750

Wentworth Castle in Yorkshire, England

Fact

A powerful Whig politician, Charles James Fox, inherited one of the largest fortunes in Georgian England, but he loved to gamble. Fox went bankrupt twice, had his furniture confiscated by bailiffs, and by the time of his death had gambled away £200 000 – perhaps £18 million in today's money.

Leisure and entertainment

The Georgian aristocracy and gentry certainly knew how to enjoy themselves. Horseracing, card games, hunting, theatre, the opera, and – most notably – gambling were all popular amongst the Georgian elite. They drank and gambled at exclusive London clubs such as Brooks' and White's, and visited fashionable holiday towns such as Brighton and Bath, which are still famous for their fine Georgian architecture.

For half of the year, from January to June, Parliament was in session, so the aristocracy decamped from their country estates to their smart London townhouses. Known as the **'season'**, this period was accompanied by a whirl of glamorous parties and events. A collection of fields to the west of London where the May Fair took place each year, had recently been developed by its owner Sir Thomas Grosvenor into townhouses. This new development became known as Mayfair, and at its centre lay Grosvenor Square, the most fashionable address in London.

Scene from 'Marriage à la mode', a series of paintings by William Hogarth satirising aristocratic life

Having the right tastes in fashion and art was very important to the Georgian aristocracy, and they often acted as patrons to young writers and artists. For the sons of Britain's aristocracy, the best way to finish their education was to undertake a **'Grand Tour'** of Europe. Lasting around two years, young aristocratic men on a Grand Tour learned about the culture and history of Europe – in particular Italy.

While travelling, these young aristocrats bought artefacts from Ancient Rome, fashionable European clothes, and paintings by celebrated artists, such as the Venetian painter Canaletto. However, many young aristocrats set free in Europe took a different path, spending their money on drinking, gambling and womanising instead.

Samuel Johnson

The son of a poor bookseller from Lichfield, Samuel Johnson worked his way to the University of Oxford and onwards to becoming one of the greatest writers in the English language. He was famously ugly, and had lots of nervous tics. However, because he was so witty and intelligent, his company was highly sought after by the Georgian aristocracy, in particular his lifelong friend and biographer James Boswell.

After 10 years of work, Johnson published one of the first English language dictionaries in 1755. It contained the definitions for 40 000 words. These included some amusing entries. Johnson defined 'dull' as "Not exhilarating; not delightful; as, to make dictionaries is dull work".

Check your understanding

1. How many aristocratic peers were there in England at the beginning of the 18th century?
2. How did the aristocracy still have power over the House of Commons?
3. Why did the aristocracy spend half of the year in London, and half of the year in their stately homes?
4. What would young aristocrats do while they undertook the Grand Tour?
5. What achievement is Samuel Johnson best remembered for?

Unit 6: Georgian Britain
Poverty, violence and crime

While the power and wealth of Georgian Britain flowed to the aristocracy, many in Britain's towns and cities lived lives of poverty, violence and crime.

Some of the worst poverty was to be found in London, where people moved to find work, but sudden joblessness could make them destitute. The poorest families lived in single, unfurnished rooms, with no running water or sanitation.

For those who could not afford a room, vagrancy was the only alternative. It was not uncommon to find dead bodies on the streets of major cities, particularly on cold winter mornings. In 1753, a writer called Henry Fielding described the streets of London as "oppressed with hunger, cold, nakedness and filth… There is not a street that does not swarm all day with beggars, and all night with thieves".

Many of the poor drowned their sorrows with a newly popular drink called gin. Cheap and strong, it was said that in 1730s London there was a shop selling gin for every 11 people. George II's Vice-Chamberlain observed "the whole town of London swarmed with drunken people from morning till night." Gin was blamed for a host of social problems, from violence and robberies to murders, irreligion and child mortality. This can be seen in the vivid print *Gin Lane*, created by William Hogarth in 1751 (see box).

William Hogarth's print 'Gin Lane', showing the social consequences of gin addiction amongst the Georgian poor

Whenever Parliament tried to control the trade of gin with licensing acts, the people of London would riot. In 1736, Parliament introduced an annual £50 licence which shopkeepers had to buy in order to sell gin. In response, angry crowds spread through London chanting "No gin, no king!". The 1751 Gin Act succeeded in placing a tax on the drink, and began a decline in gin's popularity.

Law and order

Georgian Britain could be a strikingly violent place. The right to bear arms was enshrined in the 1689 Bill of Rights, so that the Protestant population could arm themselves against the Catholic threat. Members of the aristocracy commonly carried swords, and pistols were easy to purchase. As the century went on, these weapons were increasingly used for violent crime.

There was no organised police force in Georgian Britain. While smaller towns and villages were able to govern themselves, in the growing towns and cities violent crime became a severe problem. Criminals would break

Fact

Even dead bodies would be stolen in Georgian England. 'Body snatchers' robbed newly dug graves, and sold the corpses to trainee doctors and anatomists who used them for dissections.

into houses, rob passers-by on the streets, and steal cargo from ships. Crime waves often followed the end of foreign wars, when industry would slump due to the army no longer needing supplies, and soldiers would return home unable to find jobs.

For criminals facing trial, Georgian prisons were frequently likened to hell on earth. Many prisons were run as private, profit-making organisations, so prisoners were kept in horrific conditions to keep costs low. Human waste lined the floors of overcrowded and windowless cells, which were freezing cold in the winter and unbearably hot in the summer. Newgate was the most notorious of all London's prisons. During the 18th century, Newgate suffered repeated outbreaks of typhus, a fatal disease spread by lice. Prisoners would often escape by breaking through the floor of their cells and exiting through the sewer.

Platform and gallows at Newgate Prison, Old Bailey, City of London, 1783

Highwaymen

The 18th century saw an increase in **highwaymen**: armed robbers on horseback who attacked people travelling in **stagecoaches** along dark, empty roads. The use of cheques only became common during the second half of the century, so people often had to carry large sums of money in person. Travellers came to dread the sound of galloping hooves and pistol shots, followed by the infamous cry "Stand and Deliver! Your money or your life!"

The most well known highwayman was Dick Turpin. Today he is remembered as a dashing hero, but in reality he was a convicted murderer who terrorised the roads of Essex until he was hanged at York in 1739.

Grave and headstone of Dick Turpin

William Hogarth

Perhaps the greatest artist of Georgian Britain was William Hogarth. His father was an impoverished Latin teacher, and Hogarth spent his childhood drawing caricatures of London street life. He came to specialise in **satirical** cartoons, often criticising the moral failings of Georgian society, such as its addiction to gin.

Hogarth's works liked to tell a story. His series of paintings known as *A Rake's Progress* follows the son of a wealthy merchant who wastes all of his money on fine clothes, women and gambling, before becoming bankrupt and being sent to a mental asylum.

Check your understanding

1. In cities such as London, what sort of conditions did the poorest in society have to live in?
2. What happened when Parliament tried to control the sale of gin during the 18th century?
3. Why was crime particularly serious during the Georgian period following the end of foreign wars?
4. Why did 18th century highwaymen target people who were travelling?
5. What were conditions like in 18th century prisons?

Unit 6: Georgian Britain
Knowledge organiser

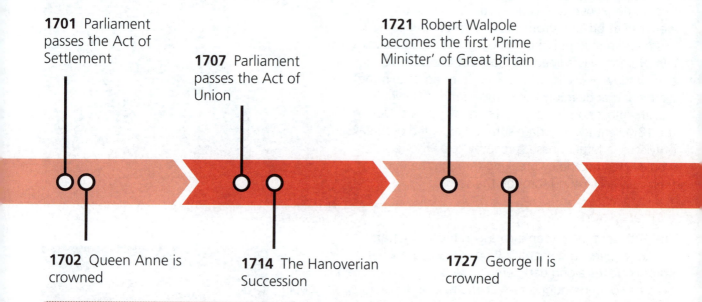

1701 Parliament passes the Act of Settlement

1707 Parliament passes the Act of Union

1721 Robert Walpole becomes the first 'Prime Minister' of Great Britain

1702 Queen Anne is crowned

1714 The Hanoverian Succession

1727 George II is crowned

Key vocabulary

10 Downing Street Traditional home of the English Prime Minister since the reign of George I

Act of Settlement A law passed in 1701 ensuring that a Protestant would succeed Queen Anne

Act of Union A law which united England and Scotland in 1707, and created Great Britain

Aristocracy The government of a country by an elite class, often with hereditary titles

Clan Ancient family from the Highlands of Scotland

Claymore A traditional Scottish sword

Darien Scheme A failed attempt by the Scottish government to establish a Caribbean trading colony

Fort George A large British barracks built in the Scottish Highlands following Jacobite defeat

Gout An illness caused by heavy eating or drinking, which causes joints to become swollen

Grand Tour Journey taken by upper class young men to experience the art and culture of Europe

Great Britain A name given to the island comprising England, Wales and Scotland

Hanoverians A royal dynasty that ruled England from 1714 until 1837

Highlands A sparsely populated area of northern Scotland known for its mountainous landscape

Highwaymen Armed robbers on horseback who attacked people travelling in stagecoaches

House of Commons The 'lower house' in Parliament, where seats go to MPs elected by the people

House of Lords The 'upper house' in Parliament, where seats are inherited by members of the peerage

Jacobite Supporters of the Stuart claim to the throne, following the exile of James II

Minister A politician with a central role within the nation's government

Parliamentary government A political system where ministers must be chosen from the most powerful party in Parliament

Peer A member of the House of Lords who, for most of English history, were from the nobility

Prime Minister The most senior post in the British government, first held by Sir Robert Walpole

Satirical Using humour to criticise human failings, often in the context of politics

Season A six-month period when Parliament was in session and the aristocracy came to London

Share A portion of a company that can be bought, bringing with it a portion of the profits

1739
The highwayman Dick Turpin is hanged in York

1746 The Battle of Culloden

1751 Parliament pass the Gin Act

1745 Bonnie Prince Charlie leads a Jacobite uprising

1755 Samuel Johnson publishes his dictionary of the English language

Key people

Bonnie Prince Charlie The last Stuart claimant to Britain's throne, and leader of a failed rebellion in 1745

Dick Turpin Legendary 18th century highwayman from Essex

Duke of Cumberland Son of George II, nicknamed 'the Butcher' for his suppression of the Highlands

George I The first Hanoverian King of England, previously a minor German prince

Queen Anne The last Stuart monarch, who created the union between England and Scotland

Robert Walpole A major Georgian statesman, generally seen as Britain's first Prime Minister

Samuel Johnson Famous Georgian writer, author of one of the first dictionaries of the English language

William Hogarth English satirical artist, his best known works are 'Gin Lane' and 'A Rake's Progress'.

Key vocabulary

Stagecoach A horse drawn carriage used for long distance travel

Suppression A dominant political power limiting the freedom and activity of a group of people

Tartan Traditional patterned cloth of Scotland, often used to make kilts

The South Sea Bubble An economic disaster caused by the sudden drop in share price of a colonial trading company

Tories A political party which originally formed to protect the power of the king

Union Jack Nickname for the national flag of Great Britain

Whigs A political party which originally formed to limit the power of the king

Quiz questions

Chapter 1: Creation of Great Britain

1. How many children did Queen Anne have, all of whom did not survive childhood?
2. Who was threatening to claim the English throne, due to Queen Anne's lack of children?
3. What law was passed in 1701 to ensure that a Protestant would succeed Queen Anne?
4. Which country was furious with the 1701 law, and declared that they would choose their own monarch?
5. What failed attempt to establish a Caribbean trading colony left the country almost bankrupt?
6. In what year was the Act of Union passed?
7. Who became king of England in 1714?
8. How many times had this new king previously visited England prior to 1714?
9. How many Catholics had a better claim to the throne than the man who became king in 1714?
10. What name is given to the royal dynasty that ruled England from 1714 until 1837?

Chapter 2: Parliamentary government

1. Which Georgian statesman is generally seen as Britain's first Prime Minister?
2. What economic disaster occurred in 1720?
3. Where did Britain's first Prime Minister spend six months as a young man?
4. What did George I give Britain's first Prime Minister, which remains part of the position today?
5. Who succeeded George I in 1727?
6. Aside from keeping taxes low, what was Britain's first Prime Minister's main ambition?
7. How was the king's power to choose his government ministers constrained?
8. What names are given to the two 'Houses' of the British Parliament?
9. How were members of the 'lower' House of Parliament chosen?
10. What two rival political parties had emerged by this time?

Chapter 3: Jacobite uprising

1. Where did the term 'Jacobite' come from?
2. Which royal dynasty did the Jacobites support?
3. In what year did the last Jacobite uprising begin?
4. Where in Britain was the support for the Jacobite cause the strongest?
5. What nickname was given to the Jacobite leader Charles Edward Stuart?
6. What English town did the Jacobite army reach, before turning back towards Scotland?
7. Where was the Jacobite army defeated in 1746?
8. Who defeated the Jacobites, and earned the nickname 'the Butcher'?
9. What term is given to the British response to the Jacobite rising in Scotland?
10. What did the British build outside Inverness to ensure that no more rebellions could take place again?

Chapter 4: Georgian aristocracy

1. What term is sometimes given to the 18th century due to the power of the nobility?
2. Which class was in the decline during the 18th century, compared with the aristocracy?
3. What were members of the House of Lords, almost always from the nobility, called?
4. Which stately home, built by the 2nd Marquess of Rockingham, is the largest in Britain?
5. In which two fashionable London clubs did the aristocracy like to drink and gamble?
6. In which fashionable Georgian holiday town can Georgian architecture still be seen today?
7. What was the six-month period when Parliament was in session and the aristocracy came to London called?
8. What were the journeys taken by upper class young men to experience the art and culture of Europe called?
9. Which famous Georgian writer published one of the first dictionaries of the English language in 1755?
10. How many word definitions did his dictionary contain?

Chapter 5: Poverty, violence and crime

1. What drink became increasingly popular amongst the poor during the 18th century?
2. In what year did Parliament pass an act to tax the sale of this drink?
3. Which artist gained fame for his depictions of poverty and alcohol addiction in Georgian London?
4. What series of paintings following the son of a wealthy merchant who ends up in a mental asylum did he create?
5. What term is given to the use of humour to criticise human failings – common in Georgian art?
6. The end of what would often cause crime waves in Georgian Britain?
7. What right, enshrined in the Bill of Rights, contributed to the crime of this period?
8. What was the most notorious London prison during this period?
9. What form of transport did highwaymen target on empty roads at night?
10. Which well-known Georgian highwayman was hanged in York in 1739?

Oxford, May 1970.

K.w

£3.50

Jay Crispin Wilson.

KCL.